THE SLOW LIVING HANDBOOK

Discovering Joy in Simplicity

Leah Luthor

ATI Publishing

CONTENTS

INTRODUCTION

In a world that seems to spin faster each day, where constant busyness and digital distractions prevail, it's easy to feel overwhelmed and disconnected from what truly matters. This book is an invitation to embark on a transformative journey —a journey that will lead you back to the essence of life, to a place of presence, purpose, and profound joy.

In these pages, you will discover the profound philosophy of slow living—a mindset that encourages us to pause, breathe, and fully engage with the richness of each moment. Slow living is not about merely reducing the pace of our lives; it's a mindful and intentional approach to embracing simplicity, cultivating well-being, and savoring the beauty in every aspect of our existence.

At its core, slow living is a gentle rebellion against the societal pressure to constantly achieve, accumulate, and conform. It's a conscious choice to step off the fast track and reevaluate what truly matters to us as individuals. It's about embracing a life that prioritizes connection, gratitude, and the pursuit of meaningful experiences.

"The Slow Living Handbook" is designed to be your compass on this journey—a guiding light that illuminates the path toward a more balanced, purposeful, and fulfilling life. Each chapter offers practical insights, inspiring stories, and actionable steps to help you integrate slow living principles into your everyday reality.

Together, we will explore the power of mindfulness, the importance of creating a tranquil home environment, and the joy of savoring slow food. We will delve into the significance of self-care, nurturing meaningful relationships, and immersing ourselves in the wonders of nature. We will also address the challenges of balancing work and leisure, navigating the digital age, and cultivating inner stillness.

Throughout this book, you will find gentle reminders to slow down, to breathe deeply, and to savor the simple pleasures that surround you. It's an invitation to awaken your senses, to be fully present in each moment, and to embrace the inherent beauty of a life lived consciously.

Remember, embracing slow living is not about perfection or rigid rules. It's a personal journey—a journey that invites you to listen to your own heart, to honor your unique needs, and to find the rhythm that resonates with your soul.

As you turn the pages of "The Slow Living Handbook," allow yourself the gift of reflection, of deep introspection, and of intentional action. May this book empower you to create a life that is aligned with your deepest values, a life filled with joy, fulfillment, and an abiding sense of peace.

Are you ready to embark on this transformative journey? Let us begin.

CHAPTER 1: UNVEILING SLOW LIVING

I n a world dominated by the relentless pursuit of progress, success, and instant gratification, the art of slow living stands as a silent rebel—a gentle resistance against the chaos that engulfs us. As we step into the realm of slow living, we uncover a transformative philosophy that challenges the hurried pace of modern life and beckons us to embrace a more deliberate, mindful, and meaningful existence.

In this chapter, we embark on a journey of discovery, delving into the origins, principles, and profound significance of this intentional lifestyle. This chapter serves as a portal, opening the door to a world where time is savored, not squandered, and where presence becomes the greatest gift we can offer ourselves.

As we explore the roots of slow living, we encounter pioneers who dared to question the status quo and sought an alternative way of being. From the early advocates who rebelled against the Industrial Revolution's frantic rhythm to the modern proponents who champion a return to simplicity, each thread of this tapestry weaves a narrative of conscious living.

The principles of slow living extend far beyond the mere art of slowing down. We investigate the holistic nature of this lifestyle, recognizing that it touches every aspect of our being—our choices, our values, and our sense of purpose. We confront the notion that busyness is a badge of honor, challenging the illusion that a life brimming with activity equates to a life well-lived.

In this chapter, we take a magnifying glass to the concept of success, reframing it in a way that aligns with our deepest desires and aspirations. We explore the significance of defining our own version of success—one that revolves around fulfillment, contentment, and genuine connection.

As we immerse ourselves in the essence of slow living, we are invited to question the societal norms that have conditioned us to measure time in seconds, productivity in tasks completed, and happiness in possessions amassed. We pause to reflect on the rush that permeates our days, recognizing the toll it takes on our well-being and relationships.

Unveiling slow living is an act of liberation—a liberation from the relentless pursuit of more, from the constant pressure to keep up, and from the never-ending to-do lists that dominate our lives. It is an opportunity to embrace stillness, to cultivate inner wisdom, and to find solace in the simplicity of existence.

As we journey through this chapter, let us approach the concept of slow living with an open heart and an inquisitive mind. Let us uncover the treasures hidden within its folds and allow its gentle wisdom to permeate our lives. For in this exploration of slow living, we may find the keys to unlocking a life that is abundant in presence, purpose, and profound joy.

Exploring the Origins and Principles of Slow Living

The roots of slow living stretch deep into history, but it wasn't until the late 1980s that the term "slow living" emerged as a counter-cultural movement. Born as a response to the fast-paced, consumer-driven society, slow living seeks to reclaim time, reconnect with the natural rhythms of life, and foster a deeper sense of well-being.

One of the key influences on the slow living movement was the concept of "Slow Food," which originated in Italy in 1986. This movement, led by Carlo Petrini, aimed to preserve local culinary traditions, promote sustainable agriculture, and encourage the enjoyment of meals as a shared experience. Slow Food became a catalyst for a broader shift towards a more intentional and mindful way of living.

Slow living, at its core, is grounded in several fundamental principles that guide its philosophy and practice:

Mindful Presence
Slow living invites us to be fully present in each moment, to savor the richness of our experiences, and to cultivate a heightened awareness of the world around us. By practicing mindfulness, we awaken to the beauty and wonder of everyday life.

Slowing Down
Embracing slow living means deliberately slowing down the pace of our lives. It challenges the idea that faster is always better and encourages us to find a sustainable rhythm that allows for rest, reflection, and true connection.

Intentional Living
Slow living calls us to live with intention and purpose. It prompts us to question our choices, to align our actions with our values, and to prioritize what truly matters to us. It encourages us to let go of what is extraneous and focus on what brings us joy and fulfillment.

Simplicity and Minimalism
Slow living embraces simplicity and minimalism, advocating for

a less cluttered and more meaningful existence. By decluttering our physical spaces and reducing our material possessions, we create room for clarity, freedom, and a greater appreciation of the essentials.

Connection and Community
Slow living emphasizes the importance of building and nurturing meaningful relationships. It encourages us to connect deeply with our loved ones, to foster a sense of belonging within our communities, and to prioritize human connection over digital distractions.

Nature and Sustainability
Slow living reminds us of our interconnectedness with the natural world. It encourages us to cultivate a harmonious relationship with nature, to prioritize sustainable practices, and to recognize the value of living in balance with the Earth.

Well-being and Self-care
Slow living recognizes the importance of self-care and well-being as foundational elements of a fulfilling life. It encourages us to prioritize rest, relaxation, and self-reflection, allowing us to recharge and nourish our minds, bodies, and spirits.

By exploring the origins and principles of slow living, we gain insight into the values and ideals that underpin this intentional way of being. It is an invitation to reflect on our own lives, to reassess our priorities, and to consider how we can embrace a slower, more purposeful path—one that brings us closer to the essence of what it means to truly live.

Recognizing the Need to Step Away from the Culture of Busyness

In today's fast-paced and hyperconnected world, busyness has become a badge of honor—a symbol of productivity and success. We live in a society that glorifies being constantly on the go, where being busy is often equated with being important or accomplished. However, beneath the surface lies a profound truth: the culture of busyness is taking a toll on our well-being and eroding the quality of our lives.

As we immerse ourselves in a never-ending stream of tasks, commitments, and obligations, we can easily lose sight of what truly matters. We find ourselves caught in a relentless cycle of busyness, constantly striving to do more, achieve more, and be more. In the process, we sacrifice our precious time, our mental and emotional well-being, and our ability to be fully present in the moment.

Recognizing the need to step away from the culture of busyness is the first step towards embracing slow living. It requires us to challenge the deeply ingrained beliefs and societal expectations that demand constant activity and productivity. It asks us to question whether our busyness is truly serving us or if it is merely a means of distraction and avoidance.

By taking a moment to pause and reflect, we can begin to unravel the layers of busyness that have entangled our lives. We may realize that the pursuit of busyness is driven by external pressures —the fear of missing out, the need for validation, or the desire to conform to societal norms. We start to see that our worth is not measured by the number of tasks we check off our to-do lists but by the depth of our connections, the moments of joy we experience, and the alignment of our actions with our values.

Stepping away from the culture of busyness is an act of reclaiming our time, our energy, and our autonomy. It allows us to create space for rest, reflection, and self-care. It opens up the possibility of experiencing a greater sense of fulfillment and contentment in our lives.

Embracing slow living requires setting boundaries and learning to prioritize our well-being. It means giving ourselves permission to say no, to opt out of the constant hustle, and to carve out time for activities that nourish our souls. It involves letting go of the fear of missing out and embracing the joy of missing out—the joy of being fully present in the moment and immersed in what truly matters to us.

Stepping away from the culture of busyness is not a one-time event but an ongoing commitment. It requires conscious effort and a willingness to challenge societal norms. As we shift our focus from busyness to presence, from quantity to quality, we begin to discover the beauty in simplicity, the joy in stillness, and the freedom in embracing a slower, more intentional way of living.

By recognizing the need to step away from the culture of busyness, we reclaim our power to shape our lives according to our own values and aspirations. We invite a greater sense of balance, purpose, and meaning into our existence. So, let us pause, take a deep breath, and embark on the journey towards slow living —a journey that promises a more meaningful, fulfilling, and authentic way of being.

Redefining Success and Embracing a More Balanced Approach to Life

In the realm of slow living, the conventional definition of success undergoes a profound transformation. It transcends the narrow confines of material wealth, status, and external achievements and expands to encompass a holistic and balanced way of being.

Embracing slow living invites us to redefine success on our own terms. It encourages us to shift our focus from the relentless pursuit of external markers of achievement to a deeper exploration of what truly brings us joy, fulfillment, and a sense of purpose. It asks us to question the societal narratives that equate success with busyness, accumulation, and constant growth.

When we embrace a more balanced approach to life, we recognize that success extends far beyond our professional endeavors. It encompasses our relationships, our well-being, our personal growth, and our connection with the world around us. It acknowledges that true success lies in nurturing our inner lives, fostering meaningful connections, and living in harmony with our values.

Slow living prompts us to reflect on what truly matters to us, allowing us to redefine our own measures of success. It invites us to ask ourselves: What brings us joy and fulfillment? What do we value most in life? How do we want to contribute to the world? These contemplations guide us towards a more authentic and balanced understanding of success.

Embracing a more balanced approach to life means honoring our well-being. It reminds us that success is not synonymous with burning ourselves out or sacrificing our physical, mental, and emotional health. Slow living encourages us to prioritize self-care, rest, and rejuvenation. It reminds us that our well-being is a fundamental pillar of success, enabling us to show up fully in all areas of our lives.

Furthermore, a balanced approach to life involves cultivating and nurturing our relationships. Slow living invites us to invest time and energy in fostering meaningful connections with our loved ones, friends, and community. It reminds us that true success lies in the richness of our relationships and the support we offer and receive.

Embracing a balanced approach to life also entails honoring our passions and cultivating a sense of purpose. Slow living encourages us to engage in activities that align with our values, passions, and interests. It urges us to pursue our creative endeavors, hobbies, and personal growth. By aligning our actions with our authentic selves, we cultivate a sense of purpose that brings fulfillment and a deep sense of success.

Redefining success and embracing a more balanced approach to life requires a shift in mindset and a willingness to challenge societal expectations. It calls for introspection, self-reflection, and a commitment to living in alignment with our values. Slow living teaches us that true success is not measured by external accolades, but by the depth of our experiences, the authenticity of our connections, and the alignment of our lives with what truly matters.

As we embrace slow living, we embark on a journey towards a more balanced and fulfilling life—one that celebrates our unique path, honors our well-being, nurtures our relationships, and enables us to make a meaningful contribution to the world. It is a journey that invites us to redefine success and create a life of harmony, purpose, and joy.

CHAPTER 2: CULTIVATING MINDFUL AWARENESS

I n our modern world, where distractions abound and the pace of life seems to accelerate by the day, the practice of cultivating mindful awareness becomes increasingly vital. In this chapter, we delve into the transformative power of mindfulness and explore how it can enrich our lives and deepen our connection to the present moment.

Mindful awareness is the practice of intentionally paying attention to the present moment with an attitude of curiosity, acceptance, and non-judgment. It is about fully engaging our senses, our thoughts, and our emotions in the here and now, rather than dwelling in the past or getting lost in the worries of the future.

In this fast-paced era, our minds often wander, jumping from one thought to another, constantly pulled in different directions. We find ourselves multitasking, rushing through tasks, and missing out on the richness of the present moment. But by cultivating mindful awareness, we reclaim our ability to fully experience life as it unfolds.

Through the practice of mindfulness, we develop a heightened sense of presence, anchoring ourselves in the here and now. We become attuned to the subtleties of our experiences—the sights, sounds, tastes, smells, and sensations that surround us. By bringing our attention to the present moment, we awaken to the beauty and wonder that exist in even the simplest of moments.

Cultivating mindful awareness goes beyond the act of being present; it extends to the quality of our attention. It involves approaching our experiences with openness, curiosity, and non-judgment. We observe our thoughts and emotions without getting swept away by them, allowing them to come and go like passing clouds in the sky. Through this practice, we develop a sense of inner spaciousness and freedom from the grip of our habitual patterns of thinking.

Mindful awareness also allows us to develop a deeper understanding of ourselves. By observing our thoughts, emotions, and bodily sensations without judgment, we gain insight into our patterns, biases, and conditioned responses. This self-awareness empowers us to make conscious choices, break free from unhelpful habits, and cultivate a greater sense of authenticity and well-being.

In this chapter, we will explore various techniques and practices to cultivate mindful awareness in our daily lives. We will learn how to integrate mindfulness into our routines, whether through formal meditation practices or by infusing mindfulness into our everyday activities. We will discover the power of breath awareness, body scans, and other mindfulness techniques to anchor ourselves in the present moment.

Moreover, we will delve into the benefits of mindful awareness, ranging from reducing stress and anxiety to enhancing our ability to respond skillfully to life's challenges. We will also explore how mindful awareness can foster deeper connections in our relationships, improve our emotional well-being, and increase our overall sense of fulfillment.

By immersing ourselves in the practice of cultivating mindful awareness, we embark on a journey of self-discovery and transformation. We tap into the innate wisdom that resides within us and learn to navigate life's ups and downs with grace and resilience. Ultimately, cultivating mindful awareness opens the door to a more conscious, meaningful, and joyful way of living.

Embracing Mindfulness as a Pathway to Presence and Inner Calm

In our fast-paced and often chaotic world, finding moments of stillness and inner calm can feel like a rare luxury. However, through the practice of mindfulness, we can cultivate a deep sense of presence and tap into a wellspring of inner peace amidst the busyness of life.

Mindfulness is the art of intentionally directing our attention to the present moment, with a non-judgmental and accepting attitude. It is about fully immersing ourselves in the here and now, without getting caught up in regrets about the past or worries about the future. By embracing mindfulness, we invite a profound shift in our relationship with ourselves and the world around us.

One of the primary benefits of mindfulness is its ability to bring us into the present moment. Too often, our minds are preoccupied with thoughts and concerns, pulling us away from fully experiencing what is happening right now. We might be physically present, but our minds wander elsewhere, missing out on the richness of our immediate experience.

Through the practice of mindfulness, we learn to anchor our attention in the present moment, whether it be through focusing on our breath, observing our bodily sensations, or tuning in to the sounds and sights around us. By doing so, we awaken to the beauty and depth that exists in each passing moment. We become fully engaged with our experiences, noticing the subtleties, and savoring the simple joys that might have otherwise gone unnoticed.

As we embrace mindfulness, we begin to cultivate a sense of inner calm. By acknowledging our thoughts and emotions without judgment, we create space for them to arise and dissipate. We no longer get entangled in the web of our racing thoughts or overwhelmed by our emotions. Instead, we observe them with a gentle curiosity, allowing them to pass through our awareness like waves in the ocean.

Through this process, we realize that we are not defined by our thoughts or emotions. We are the observers, the witness to our inner landscape. This recognition brings a newfound sense of peace and tranquility. We become less reactive to external circumstances and more anchored in our inner wisdom and resilience. Mindfulness becomes a refuge, a sanctuary of stillness amidst the storms of life.

Embracing mindfulness as a pathway to presence and inner calm requires practice and dedication. It is not a quick fix or an instant solution. It is a lifelong journey of self-discovery and self-awareness. We learn to cultivate mindfulness through formal meditation practices, such as sitting or walking meditation, as well as through integrating mindfulness into our daily activities.

By incorporating mindfulness into our lives, we create moments of pause and reflection. We bring mindful awareness to even the simplest activities, such as eating, walking, or washing dishes. We savor the sensations, the textures, and the flavors of each experience. We become fully present, imbuing even the most mundane tasks with a sense of sacredness and joy.

The practice of mindfulness opens up a world of possibilities. It allows us to navigate the ups and downs of life with greater ease and equanimity. It deepens our connection to ourselves and others, fostering compassion, empathy, and understanding. It nurtures our well-being, reducing stress, anxiety, and burnout. It invites us to live fully, embracing each moment as an opportunity for growth and transformation.

So, let us embark on this journey of embracing mindfulness as a pathway to presence and inner calm. Let us cultivate the art of being fully present in our lives, savoring each moment, and discovering the boundless peace that resides within us. Through the practice of mindfulness, we can create a more harmonious, fulfilling, and joyful way of being in the world.

Practicing Gratitude and Finding Joy in Everyday Moments

In the hustle and bustle of our lives, it is all too easy to overlook the simple blessings and moments of joy that surround us. We get caught up in our ambitions, worries, and to-do lists, often forgetting to pause and appreciate the richness of our lives. However, by cultivating the practice of gratitude and consciously seeking out joy in everyday moments, we can profoundly transform our perception of the world and infuse our lives with greater contentment and fulfillment.

Gratitude is the practice of intentionally recognizing and appreciating the goodness in our lives. It is about shifting our focus from what is lacking or challenging to what we already have and cherish. When we cultivate gratitude, we train our minds to notice the small miracles and blessings that are present each day, even amidst difficulties.

Practicing gratitude starts with cultivating awareness. We begin by consciously directing our attention to the present moment, observing our experiences with openness and curiosity. We can create a gratitude journal, where we write down three things we are grateful for each day. It could be as simple as a beautiful sunrise, a kind word from a friend, or a moment of laughter with loved ones. By acknowledging and expressing gratitude for these everyday moments, we begin to shift our perspective and rewire our brains to focus on the positive aspects of our lives.

As we deepen our practice of gratitude, we start to notice a profound shift in our well-being. We become more attuned to the beauty and abundance that surrounds us. We develop a heightened sense of appreciation for the people, experiences, and resources that support and nourish us. Gratitude becomes a lens through which we view the world, cultivating a sense of awe, wonder, and humility.

In addition to practicing gratitude, we can actively seek out joy in everyday moments. Joy can be found in the simplest of experiences—a warm cup of tea, the sound of birds chirping, the touch of a loved one's hand. By cultivating mindfulness and presence, we open ourselves up to the joy that exists in each moment, no matter how seemingly insignificant.

To find joy in everyday moments, we can engage in practices such as mindful walking, where we intentionally observe and appreciate our surroundings as we take each step. We can also infuse our daily routines with moments of pleasure and presence, such as savoring a delicious meal, immersing ourselves in a creative project, or engaging in activities that bring us a sense of playfulness and delight.

Cultivating gratitude and finding joy in everyday moments not only enriches our own lives but also deepens our connections with others. When we express gratitude to those who have touched our lives, we acknowledge their impact and nurture the bonds that sustain us. When we share moments of joy with loved ones, we create lasting memories and strengthen our relationships.

Practicing gratitude and seeking joy in everyday moments is a conscious choice—a shift in perspective that requires dedication and awareness. It is a reminder to slow down, be present, and cultivate a sense of wonder and appreciation for the preciousness of life. By incorporating these practices into our daily lives, we open ourselves up to a world filled with gratitude, joy, and a deeper sense of meaning.

So, let us embark on this journey of cultivating gratitude and finding joy in everyday moments. Let us nurture the seeds of gratitude within us, allowing them to blossom and illuminate our lives. Let us awaken to the richness and beauty that surround us, embracing the gift of each moment with a heart filled with gratitude and a spirit infused with joy.

CHAPTER 3: CREATING A TRANQUIL HOME

Our homes are more than mere physical spaces. They are havens, sanctuaries that have the power to nourish and rejuvenate us. In this chapter, we explore the art of creating a tranquil home—a space that supports our well-being, fosters a sense of peace, and invites us to slow down and savor the simple pleasures of life.

A tranquil home is not just about aesthetics or interior design trends. It is a reflection of our values, a manifestation of our desire for balance and harmony. It is a space that cultivates a sense of serenity, both in its physical environment and in the energy it emanates. It is a sanctuary where we can retreat from the noise and demands of the outside world, and reconnect with ourselves and our loved ones.

Creating a tranquil home begins with mindful intention and thoughtful choices. It involves decluttering our physical spaces, letting go of excess belongings, and creating an environment that is free from unnecessary distractions. By simplifying our surroundings, we create a sense of spaciousness and clarity, allowing us to focus on what truly matters.

A tranquil home is one that nurtures our senses and engages us on a deep level. It incorporates elements that soothe and inspire—a soft color palette, natural materials, and textures that invite touch, gentle lighting, and the soothing sounds of nature or calming music. It embraces the principles of minimalism and simplicity, allowing for open spaces and uncluttered surfaces that promote a sense of calm and tranquility.

Beyond the physical aspects, a tranquil home also considers the emotional and energetic aspects of our living spaces. It involves creating zones for different activities—areas for rest and relaxation, for work or creative pursuits, and for nourishing connections with loved ones. It embraces the power of natural elements, such as plants, to purify the air and bring vitality to our spaces. It also acknowledges the importance of natural light and fresh air in promoting a sense of well-being.

In this chapter, we will explore practical strategies and ideas for creating a tranquil home. We will delve into the art of decluttering and organizing our living spaces, finding storage solutions that promote a sense of order and ease. We will discuss the benefits of incorporating elements of nature and mindfulness into our homes, and how they can enhance our well-being and create a deeper sense of connection.

Moreover, we will explore the concept of hygge—a Danish term that encompasses coziness, comfort, and a sense of well-being. We will discover how to infuse our homes with hygge, embracing the joy of simple pleasures, creating cozy nooks, and cultivating a sense of warmth and intimacy.

By creating a tranquil home, we not only shape our physical environment but also influence our state of mind and emotional well-being. We create a sanctuary where we can recharge, find solace, and experience a deep sense of belonging. It becomes a place where we can engage in self-care practices, foster meaningful connections, and embark on the journey of slow living with intention and grace.

So, let us embark on this exploration of creating a tranquil home.

Let us transform our living spaces into sacred retreats, infused with beauty, simplicity, and a sense of serenity. By nurturing our homes as havens of tranquility, we cultivate a sanctuary that supports our journey towards a more intentional, balanced, and fulfilling way of living.

Simplifying Your Living Space and Decluttering

In our modern consumer-driven society, it's easy to accumulate an abundance of belongings. Our homes can quickly become filled with possessions, many of which we no longer need or use. This accumulation of clutter not only occupies physical space but also weighs us down mentally and emotionally. In this subchapter, we will explore the importance of simplifying our living spaces and the transformative power of decluttering.

Simplifying your living space is about consciously choosing to surround yourself with only the things that truly add value and bring you joy. It is a process of letting go of the excess and creating a space that feels spacious, organized, and conducive to a sense of calm. By simplifying, we create room for what truly matters and eliminate the distractions and burdens that clutter brings.

Decluttering is the first step in simplifying your living space. It involves systematically going through your belongings and deciding what to keep, what to donate or sell, and what to discard. It can be an emotional process, as we may have attachments to certain items or fear letting go of things we no longer use. However, decluttering provides an opportunity for growth, as we learn to detach ourselves from material possessions and focus on what truly matters in our lives.

When embarking on the decluttering journey, it's helpful to approach it with a mindset of mindfulness and intention. Take the time to reflect on your values and priorities. Consider what truly brings you joy and aligns with your current lifestyle. Let go of items that no longer serve a purpose or hold sentimental value.

By surrounding yourself with only the essentials and the things you truly cherish, you create a living space that reflects your authentic self.

There are various strategies you can employ to simplify and declutter your living space effectively. One approach is to tackle decluttering room by room or category by category. Start with one area, such as a closet or a bookshelf, and go through each item, making decisions about what to keep and what to let go of. Ask yourself whether each item brings you joy or serves a practical purpose. If not, consider passing it on to someone who may find value in it.

Another helpful method is the "one in, one out" rule. For every new item you bring into your home, commit to removing one item. This practice prevents the accumulation of unnecessary belongings and encourages mindful consumption.

As you declutter, consider the environmental impact of your actions. Whenever possible, donate or sell items that are in good condition instead of discarding them. Recycle or properly dispose of items that cannot be reused. By being mindful of the waste we generate, we contribute to a more sustainable lifestyle.

The benefits of simplifying your living space and decluttering extend far beyond the physical realm. A simplified home reduces visual noise and promotes a sense of calm and clarity. It makes cleaning and organizing easier, freeing up time and energy for the things that truly matter. A clutter-free environment can also have a positive impact on mental well-being, reducing stress and promoting a greater sense of peace and serenity.

Moreover, simplifying your living space can influence your mindset and lifestyle choices. By consciously choosing what you surround yourself with, you invite intentionality and mindfulness into your daily life. You become more aware of the choices you make and the impact they have on your overall well-being.

So, embrace the practice of simplifying your living space and decluttering. Allow it to be a transformative process that brings greater clarity, peace, and freedom into your life. By consciously curating your living environment, you create a space that supports your journey toward slow living and cultivates a sense of harmony and balance.

Designing an Environment that Promotes Relaxation and Rejuvenation

Our living spaces have a significant impact on our overall well-being. The design and layout of our homes can either contribute to stress and overwhelm or promote relaxation and rejuvenation. In this subchapter, we will explore how to intentionally design an environment that fosters a sense of calm, tranquility, and rejuvenation.

Color plays a vital role in creating a relaxing atmosphere. Soft, neutral tones such as pastels, earthy hues, and muted shades can evoke a sense of serenity and create a visually soothing environment. Consider incorporating these colors into your walls, furniture, and decor. However, keep in mind that everyone's preferences may differ, so choose colors that resonate with you personally and bring a sense of calmness.

Another essential aspect of designing a relaxing environment is lighting. Natural light is incredibly beneficial and can instantly uplift your mood. Maximize the natural light in your home by keeping windows unobstructed and using sheer curtains or blinds that allow sunlight to filter through. Additionally, consider incorporating warm, ambient lighting in the evenings, such as soft, dimmable lamps or candles, to create a cozy and peaceful atmosphere.

The arrangement and flow of furniture can greatly impact the energy and functionality of a space. Opt for an open layout that allows for easy movement and promotes a sense of spaciousness. Arrange furniture in a way that encourages conversation and connection, creating inviting spaces for relaxation and socializing.

Incorporating natural elements into your living space can create a sense of harmony and connection with the outdoors. Introduce indoor plants to add life, beauty, and a touch of nature to your home. Plants not only purify the air but also have a calming effect on our minds. Choose low-maintenance varieties that thrive indoors and consider placing them strategically throughout your home, including in areas where you spend the most time.

Textiles and fabrics also play a significant role in creating a cozy and inviting atmosphere. Opt for soft, natural materials such as cotton, linen, or wool for bedding, upholstery, and curtains. These materials not only feel luxurious but also create a tactile experience that promotes a sense of comfort and relaxation.

Consider creating dedicated spaces for relaxation and rejuvenation within your home. Designate a cozy reading nook with a comfortable chair, soft blankets, and a side table for books and beverages. Create a meditation or mindfulness corner with cushions, a yoga mat, and candles. Having these intentional spaces allows you to escape the demands of daily life and indulge in moments of self-care and reflection.

Lastly, ensure that your living space is organized and clutter-free. Clutter can create a sense of chaos and increase stress levels. Use smart storage solutions to keep your belongings organized and out of sight. By simplifying and decluttering, you create a space that feels light, airy, and conducive to relaxation.

Designing an environment that promotes relaxation and rejuvenation is a personal and ongoing process. It involves creating a space that reflects your individual preferences, needs, and desires. Take the time to assess your living space and consider how each element contributes to or detracts from a sense of tranquility. Make intentional choices that align with your vision of a relaxing home.

By intentionally designing an environment that promotes relaxation and rejuvenation, you create a sanctuary within your home—a space where you can unwind, recharge, and nurture your well-being. Your living space becomes a refuge from the external demands and stresses of life, supporting your journey toward slow living and a more balanced and fulfilling existence.

CHAPTER 4: NOURISHING SLOW FOOD

F ood is not merely fuel for our bodies; it is a source of nourishment, pleasure, and connection. In a world dominated by fast food, instant meals, and mindless eating, it is essential to reclaim our relationship with food and embrace the principles of slow food. In this chapter, we delve into the art of nourishing our bodies and souls through mindful and intentional eating.

Slow food is an approach to food that emphasizes quality, tradition, and the pleasure of savoring each bite. It is a counterbalance to the fast food culture that prioritizes convenience and speed over the inherent value of the dining experience. Slow food invites us to slow down, engage our senses, and cultivate a deeper appreciation for the food we consume.

In this chapter, we will explore the many facets of slow food and how it can enrich our lives. We will delve into the principles of sourcing and preparing whole, unprocessed ingredients, and rediscovering the joy of cooking from scratch. We will discover the benefits of supporting local and sustainable food systems, connecting us to the land and the people who produce our food.

Slow food encourages us to shift our focus from mindless eating to mindful eating—a practice that involves being fully present and engaged in the act of eating. It asks us to savor each bite, to appreciate the flavors, textures, and aromas that nourish our senses. Mindful eating also encourages us to listen to our bodies, to tune in to our hunger and fullness cues, and to cultivate a healthier relationship with food.

We will explore practical strategies for incorporating slow food into our daily lives. From planning and preparing meals with intention to creating mindful eating rituals, we will discover how to infuse our dining experiences with a deeper sense of connection, gratitude, and pleasure. We will also explore the concept of slow food communities and how coming together around the table can foster meaningful connections and cultural exchange.

Beyond nourishing our bodies, slow food nourishes our souls. It celebrates the heritage and traditions of different culinary cultures, honoring the wisdom passed down through generations. Slow food invites us to explore diverse flavors, culinary techniques, and regional specialties, expanding our culinary horizons and deepening our appreciation for the rich tapestry of global cuisine.

By embracing the principles of slow food, we reconnect with the inherent joy and nourishment that food provides. We reclaim our relationship with the earth, the seasons, and the cycles of nature that sustain us. We honor the farmers, artisans, and producers who pour their passion and care into creating wholesome and sustainable food. We savor each meal as a moment of mindfulness and gratitude, sowing the seeds of well-being, balance, and connection.

So, join us on this journey of nourishing slow food. Let us rediscover the pleasure of mindful eating, celebrate the diversity of flavors and cultures, and cultivate a deeper connection to the food we consume. By embracing the principles of slow food, we nourish not only our bodies but also our souls, fostering a more intentional, sustainable, and joyful way of living.

Embracing Mindful Eating and Savoring the Flavors of Real, Whole Foods

In our fast-paced and busy lives, it's easy to fall into the trap of mindless eating. We rush through meals, eat on the go, or consume our food while distracted by screens or other activities. However, by embracing mindful eating and savoring the flavors of real, whole foods, we can transform our relationship with food and derive greater pleasure and nourishment from every bite.

Mindful eating is the practice of bringing our full attention and awareness to the act of eating. It involves slowing down, engaging our senses, and being fully present in the moment. By cultivating mindfulness during meals, we become attuned to the experience of eating, from the flavors and textures to the sensations of hunger and satiety.

To embrace mindful eating, start by creating a calm and inviting eating environment. Set the table with care, dim the lights, and eliminate distractions such as screens or electronic devices. Create a peaceful ambiance that allows you to focus solely on the food in front of you.

Before you take your first bite, take a moment to express gratitude for the nourishment before you. Appreciate the effort that went into growing, harvesting, and preparing the food. This simple act of gratitude can shift your mindset and set the tone for a more mindful eating experience.

As you begin to eat, engage your senses fully. Observe the colors, shapes, and textures of the food on your plate. Inhale the aromas and let them awaken your taste buds. Take small, deliberate bites and chew slowly, savoring the flavors and allowing the food to fully mix with your saliva. Notice the changing tastes and textures as you chew and swallow.

Pay attention to the sensations in your body. Notice the feeling of hunger and how it evolves as you eat. Be mindful of the signals of fullness and stop eating when you feel satisfied, rather than when your plate is empty. Remember that it takes time for your brain to register satiety, so slowing down and listening to your body is crucial.

Savoring the flavors of real, whole foods is a natural consequence of mindful eating. When we choose whole, unprocessed ingredients, we are rewarded with vibrant flavors that are often lost in highly processed or pre-packaged foods. Fresh fruits and vegetables, whole grains, and quality proteins offer a spectrum of tastes that can be truly savored.

Experiment with different ingredients and cooking techniques to expand your flavor palate. Try incorporating herbs, spices, and aromatic ingredients to add depth and complexity to your dishes. Discover the joy of preparing meals from scratch, allowing you to appreciate the transformation of raw ingredients into a nourishing and delicious meal.

When we slow down and savor the flavors of real, whole foods, we not only experience greater pleasure but also foster a deeper connection to the food we eat. We become more conscious of the impact our choices have on our health, the environment, and the communities that produce our food. Mindful eating can lead to more informed choices and a greater appreciation for the integrity and sustainability of our food systems.

So, embrace the practice of mindful eating and savor the flavors of real, whole foods. Cultivate a deeper connection to your meals and the nourishment they provide. By engaging your senses and being fully present in the act of eating, you tap into the richness of the culinary experience and foster a more mindful, satisfying, and joyful relationship with food.

Exploring Local and Sustainable Food Choices

In our quest for slow living and a more mindful approach to food, one of the key principles to embrace is exploring local and sustainable food choices. By prioritizing locally sourced and sustainably produced food, we not only support our local communities but also contribute to a more environmentally conscious and resilient food system.

Local food refers to food that is grown, produced, and distributed within a relatively close proximity to where it is consumed. By choosing local food, we reduce the distance that our food travels, which in turn reduces the carbon footprint associated with transportation. Additionally, supporting local farmers and producers helps to strengthen the local economy and preserve agricultural land.

To explore local food choices, start by getting to know your local farmers' markets. These vibrant community spaces offer a wide range of fresh produce, meats, dairy products, and other locally made goods. Engage in conversations with the farmers and artisans, learn about their farming practices, and build relationships based on trust and shared values. By directly connecting with the people who grow your food, you can gain a deeper appreciation for the care and dedication that goes into producing it.

Community-supported agriculture (CSA) programs are another excellent way to access local and seasonal produce. By joining a CSA, you become a member of a farm or a cooperative, and in return, you receive a share of the farm's harvest throughout the growing season. This arrangement not only supports local farmers financially but also strengthens the relationship between consumers and producers. It allows you to experience the joys and challenges of eating with the seasons and fosters a sense of connection to the land and the agricultural rhythms.

When exploring local food choices, don't limit yourself to just fruits and vegetables. Look for local sources of meat, poultry, dairy products, and seafood as well. Seek out farmers who practice sustainable and ethical farming methods, such as pasture-raised animals or organic practices. Supporting these farmers encourages humane treatment of animals, promotes biodiversity, and reduces the use of harmful pesticides and synthetic fertilizers.

Sustainable food choices go beyond locality and encompass the entire life cycle of food production, from farm to fork. When making sustainable food choices, consider the environmental impact of your food. Look for labels such as organic, fair trade, or Rainforest Alliance certified, which indicate environmentally friendly and socially responsible practices.

Another sustainable food choice is to incorporate more plant-based meals into your diet. Plant-based eating reduces the strain on natural resources, decreases greenhouse gas emissions, and promotes a healthier and more balanced diet. Explore a variety of fruits, vegetables, grains, legumes, and plant-based proteins to create delicious and satisfying meals that are both nourishing and sustainable.

In addition to exploring local and sustainable food choices, consider reducing food waste in your own kitchen. Plan your meals mindfully, buy only what you need, and repurpose leftovers into new dishes. Composting organic waste is another way to minimize your ecological footprint and enrich the soil.

By exploring local and sustainable food choices, we become active participants in shaping a more resilient and mindful food system. We support local farmers, foster community connections, and prioritize the well-being of our planet. By choosing food that is grown and produced with care and consideration, we nourish our bodies, honor the earth, and contribute to a more sustainable future.

So, take the time to explore your local food options, seek out sustainable sources, and engage in a deeper understanding of where your food comes from. By making conscious choices, you become an agent of change, promoting a more ethical, resilient, and environmentally friendly food system.

CHAPTER 5:
PRIORITIZING
SELF-CARE

In the hustle and bustle of modern life, self-care often takes a backseat. We find ourselves constantly juggling responsibilities, meeting deadlines, and attending to the needs of others. However, in the journey of slow living, prioritizing self-care becomes an essential component of nurturing our well-being and maintaining a balanced and fulfilling life.

Self-care is not a luxury; it is a fundamental practice that allows us to recharge, rejuvenate, and show up as our best selves. It encompasses activities and habits that promote physical, mental, and emotional well-being. By prioritizing self-care, we honor ourselves, acknowledge our needs, and cultivate a deeper sense of self-compassion and self-awareness.

In this chapter, we delve into the importance of prioritizing self-care and explore various practices and strategies to integrate it into our daily lives. We recognize that self-care is not a one-size-fits-all approach but a deeply personal and individualized journey. What works for one person may not resonate with another, and that is perfectly okay. The key is to discover and embrace self-care practices that nourish and replenish our unique selves.

We will explore self-care rituals that focus on nurturing our physical well-being. This may include engaging in regular exercise, getting enough sleep, and nourishing our bodies with wholesome and nutritious foods. We will delve into the importance of rest and relaxation, as well as the benefits of activities such as yoga, meditation, and mindful movement in fostering a sense of calm and balance.

Nurturing our mental and emotional well-being is also a crucial aspect of self-care. We will explore practices such as journaling, creative expression, and mindfulness techniques that help us cultivate self-reflection, emotional resilience, and inner peace. We will delve into the power of setting boundaries, saying no when necessary, and creating space for activities that bring us joy and fulfillment.

Self-care goes beyond individual practices; it also encompasses nurturing our relationships and fostering connections with others. We will explore the importance of cultivating healthy boundaries in our relationships, prioritizing quality time with loved ones, and creating meaningful connections that enrich our lives. We will also recognize the value of seeking support when needed, whether through therapy, counseling, or simply reaching out to trusted friends or mentors.

Prioritizing self-care requires a shift in mindset and a commitment to ourselves. It requires us to let go of the guilt or the belief that self-care is selfish. In truth, prioritizing our well-being allows us to show up more fully and authentically in all areas of our lives. It enhances our ability to care for others and contribute meaningfully to our communities.

By prioritizing self-care, we send a powerful message to ourselves and to the world. We declare that our well-being matters, that we are deserving of love, compassion, and nourishment. We create a foundation of self-care that enables us to navigate the challenges of life with greater resilience, clarity, and grace.

So, join us in exploring the art of prioritizing self-care. Discover practices that resonate with your unique needs and preferences. Embrace self-compassion and make a commitment to honor yourself through intentional acts of care and nourishment. By prioritizing self-care, you embark on a transformative journey towards self-discovery, well-being, and a more balanced and fulfilling way of living.

Cultivating Self-Care Practices to Nurture Physical, Emotional, and Mental Well-Being

Self-care is a holistic practice that encompasses nurturing our physical, emotional, and mental well-being. By intentionally cultivating self-care practices in these areas, we create a solid foundation for overall wellness and a more balanced and fulfilling life. In this subchapter, we will explore various self-care practices that can support and nourish each aspect of our well-being.

Nurturing Physical Well-Being
Physical self-care involves taking care of our bodies and prioritizing activities that promote vitality, strength, and overall health. Some practices to consider include:

- Engaging in regular exercise
Find physical activities that you enjoy, whether it's jogging, dancing, practicing yoga, or participating in team sports. Choose activities that make you feel energized and help you connect with your body.

- Getting enough sleep: Adequate sleep is essential for physical and mental rejuvenation. Establish a consistent sleep routine and create a sleep-friendly environment that promotes relaxation and restful sleep.

- Nourishing your body with wholesome foods: Pay attention to the quality and variety of foods you consume. Prioritize whole, nutrient-dense foods that provide essential vitamins, minerals, and antioxidants. Listen to your body's hunger and fullness cues and practice mindful eating.

- Taking care of your physical health: Schedule regular check-ups, screenings, and preventive care appointments. Address any health concerns or issues promptly and seek professional guidance when needed.

Nurturing Emotional Well-Being

Emotional self-care involves acknowledging and attending to our emotions, cultivating self-compassion, and building emotional resilience. Some practices to consider include:

- Journaling: Set aside time to reflect on your emotions, thoughts, and experiences. Use writing as a tool for self-expression, self-discovery, and processing your feelings.

- Engaging in creative expression: Explore creative outlets such as painting, drawing, writing, or playing a musical instrument. Allow yourself the freedom to express your emotions and experiences through art.

- Practicing mindfulness and self-compassion: Cultivate present-moment awareness and non-judgmental acceptance of your thoughts and emotions. Practice self-compassion by treating yourself with kindness, understanding, and forgiveness.

- Connecting with nature: Spend time in nature, whether it's taking a walk in a park, gardening, or simply sitting outside and appreciating the natural beauty around you. Nature has a calming and grounding effect on our emotional well-being.

Nurturing Mental Well-Being

Mental self-care involves nurturing our cognitive abilities, managing stress, and promoting mental clarity and focus. Some practices to consider include:

- Meditation and mindfulness: Set aside dedicated time each day for meditation or mindfulness practices. These practices help calm the mind, increase self-awareness, and cultivate a sense of inner peace.

- Engaging in hobbies and intellectual pursuits: Pursue activities that stimulate your mind and bring you joy. This could involve reading, learning a new skill, solving puzzles, or engaging in creative projects that challenge your thinking.

- Setting boundaries: Establish clear boundaries to protect your mental well-being. Learn to say no to excessive commitments, create space for rest and relaxation, and prioritize activities that bring you mental rejuvenation.

- Seeking mental stimulation and growth: Engage in activities that expand your knowledge and stimulate your intellect. Attend workshops, seminars, or lectures on topics that interest you. Engaging in lifelong learning keeps the mind active and curious.

Remember, self-care is an ongoing practice, and what works for one person may not work for another. Explore different self-care practices and tailor them to your unique needs and preferences. The key is to prioritize self-care as a non-negotiable aspect of your daily routine, honoring your physical, emotional, and mental well-being. By cultivating self-care practices in these areas, you lay the foundation for a more balanced, fulfilled, and resilient life.

Incorporating Rest and Rejuvenation into Your Daily Routine

In our fast-paced and demanding world, rest and rejuvenation often take a backseat to our never-ending to-do lists. However, making time for rest and rejuvenation is essential for our overall well-being and is a vital component of the slow living philosophy. Rest allows us to recharge our energy, reduce stress, and cultivate a sense of inner calm and balance. In this subchapter, we will explore ways to incorporate rest and rejuvenation into your daily routine.

Prioritize sleep

Adequate sleep is a cornerstone of rest and rejuvenation. Aim for a consistent sleep schedule that allows you to get the recommended amount of sleep for your age and needs. Create a sleep-friendly environment by ensuring your bedroom is dark, quiet, and comfortable. Establish a calming bedtime routine that helps signal to your body that it's time to unwind and prepare for sleep.

Take regular breaks

Throughout the day, schedule short breaks to pause and recharge. Step away from your work or tasks, and engage in activities that promote relaxation. This could be as simple as taking a walk outside, stretching your body, or practicing deep breathing exercises. These breaks help to refresh your mind, reduce mental fatigue, and increase productivity.

Embrace the power of solitude

Carving out moments of solitude in your daily routine can be incredibly restorative. Find a quiet space where you can be alone with your thoughts, away from distractions. Engage in activities that bring you joy and peace, such as reading, journaling, or practicing mindfulness or meditation. Solitude allows you to reconnect with yourself, gain clarity, and find inner calm.

Cultivate mindful moments

Incorporate moments of mindfulness throughout your day. Mindfulness involves intentionally paying attention to the present moment with openness and non-judgment. Engage your senses and fully experience the simple pleasures of life. Whether it's savoring a cup of tea, enjoying a walk in nature, or relishing the taste of a delicious meal, these mindful moments bring you into the present and foster a sense of relaxation and appreciation.

Engage in restorative activities

Explore activities that promote rest and rejuvenation for your body and mind. This could include practicing yoga, taking soothing baths, indulging in a hobby or creative pursuit, or enjoying gentle forms of exercise like tai chi or qigong. These activities help to release tension, reduce stress, and restore your energy levels.

Disconnect from technology

Set aside dedicated time each day to disconnect from technology. Constant connectivity can be draining and overwhelming. Create tech-free zones or time blocks where you intentionally disconnect from screens and focus on offline activities that bring you joy and relaxation. This allows your mind to unwind, reduces mental clutter, and fosters a greater sense of presence and well-being.

Practice self-compassion

Remember to be kind to yourself and give yourself permission to rest. Recognize that rest and rejuvenation are essential aspects of self-care and are not indulgent or lazy. Release any guilt or pressure to constantly be productive and allow yourself the space to rest, recharge, and replenish your energy.

By incorporating rest and rejuvenation into your daily routine, you honor your need for balance, well-being, and self-care. These moments of rest not only replenish your physical and mental energy but also cultivate a deeper connection with yourself and a greater appreciation for the present moment. Embrace rest as a necessary and valuable part of your daily life, and you will experience the transformative power of true rejuvenation.

CHAPTER 6:
CULTIVATING
MEANINGFUL
CONNECTIONS

In our increasingly digital and fast-paced world, it's easy to feel disconnected from others and to long for more meaningful connections. However, cultivating genuine and nourishing relationships is an integral part of the slow living philosophy. Building and nurturing connections with others not only brings joy and fulfillment but also enriches our lives and supports our well-being. In this chapter, we will explore the importance of cultivating meaningful connections and offer insights and practices to help you foster deep and authentic relationships in your life.

Human beings are social creatures, wired for connection and belonging. Meaningful connections with others provide us with a sense of support, understanding, and shared experiences. These connections allow us to feel seen, heard, and valued, fostering a sense of belonging and meaning in our lives.

In a world that often values quantity over quality, it's important to prioritize and invest in relationships that truly matter to us. Cultivating meaningful connections involves intentional effort, presence, and vulnerability. It requires us to step away from superficial interactions and engage in deeper and more authentic ways of relating.

In this chapter, we will explore various aspects of cultivating meaningful connections. We will delve into the importance of active listening, empathy, and compassion in building stronger relationships. We will discuss the role of vulnerability and authenticity in fostering deep connections that go beyond surface-level interactions. We will also explore the value of shared experiences and the power of community in creating a sense of belonging and support.

Furthermore, we will address the challenges that may arise in building and maintaining meaningful connections, such as busyness, digital distractions, and societal pressures. We will offer practical tips and strategies to overcome these challenges and make space for authentic connections in your life.

Cultivating meaningful connections is not solely about others; it's also about deepening our connection with ourselves. By cultivating self-awareness, self-compassion, and self-acceptance, we create a strong foundation for building authentic relationships with others. As we become more attuned to our own needs, values, and boundaries, we can show up authentically in our relationships and foster connections that align with who we truly are.

In the following chapters, we will delve deeper into the various aspects of cultivating meaningful connections. Whether it's strengthening existing relationships, forming new connections, or creating a sense of community, the practices and insights shared in this chapter will guide you towards building more meaningful, fulfilling, and authentic relationships in your life. So, let us embark on this journey of cultivating meaningful connections, where true connection and genuine belonging await.

Fostering Deep and Authentic Relationships with Loved Ones

Our relationships with our loved ones—family members, partners, and close friends—are some of the most important and cherished connections in our lives. These relationships have the potential to bring us immense joy, support, and a sense of belonging. However, cultivating deep and authentic relationships requires intentional effort, nurturing, and open communication. In this subchapter, we will explore practices and insights to help you foster and strengthen these meaningful connections with your loved ones.

Prioritize quality time

In our busy lives, it's easy to get caught up in the demands of work and other responsibilities, leaving little time for our loved ones. To foster deep and authentic relationships, it's essential to prioritize quality time together. Set aside dedicated time to be fully present with your loved ones, free from distractions. Engage in activities that promote connection, such as having meaningful conversations, sharing meals, going on walks, or engaging in hobbies together.

Practice active listening

Deepening your relationships requires being fully present and actively listening to your loved ones. When someone is sharing their thoughts, feelings, or experiences, give them your undivided attention. Avoid interrupting or formulating responses in your mind. Instead, focus on understanding their perspective, validating their emotions, and showing genuine interest in what they have to say. Active listening builds trust, empathy, and a stronger connection.

Cultivate empathy and compassion

Empathy and compassion are essential qualities for fostering deep and authentic relationships. Seek to understand and empathize with the experiences, challenges, and emotions of your loved ones. Put yourself in their shoes and offer support and understanding. Practice compassion by being kind, patient, and forgiving. This creates a safe and nurturing space where your loved ones feel valued, accepted, and supported.

Communicate openly and honestly

Effective communication is the foundation of any healthy relationship. Cultivate open and honest communication with your loved ones, creating an environment where thoughts, feelings, and concerns can be expressed without judgment or fear of rejection. Share your own vulnerabilities and encourage your loved ones to do the same. Honest and transparent communication builds trust, deepens understanding, and strengthens the emotional bond.

Show appreciation and gratitude

Expressing appreciation and gratitude to your loved ones strengthens the connection and reinforces the positive aspects of your relationship. Regularly acknowledge and celebrate their presence, contributions, and qualities that you value. Simple gestures of gratitude, such as saying "thank you" or leaving notes of appreciation, go a long way in nurturing love and appreciation within the relationship.

Nurture shared experiences

Shared experiences create lasting memories and deepen the bond with your loved ones. Engage in activities that allow you to connect, have fun, and create meaningful moments together. This could involve traveling, exploring nature, pursuing shared hobbies, or engaging in new adventures. These shared experiences foster a sense of connection, strengthen the emotional bond, and create a shared history that can be cherished.

Respect individuality and boundaries

While cultivating deep relationships, it's important to respect the individuality and boundaries of your loved ones. Each person has their own unique needs, preferences, and personal space. Allow space for personal growth, interests, and independence within the relationship. Respect boundaries and communicate openly about them, ensuring that each person feels valued and respected for who they are.

Remember, fostering deep and authentic relationships is an ongoing journey that requires patience, understanding, and effort. It involves both giving and receiving support, love, and care. By implementing these practices and insights, you can cultivate relationships with your loved ones that are built on trust, intimacy, and a shared sense of purpose. These connections will enrich your life, bring you joy, and provide a source of strength and support as you navigate the journey of slow living.

Embracing mindful communication and presence in your interactions

In our fast-paced and interconnected world, mindful communication and presence in our interactions have become increasingly important. With the constant distractions and demands of technology, it's easy to fall into the trap of fragmented conversations, superficial connections, and a lack of genuine presence.

Embracing mindful communication means bringing our full attention and awareness to the present moment and to the person or people we are engaging with. It involves setting aside our distractions, judgments, and preconceived notions, and truly listening to understand, rather than simply waiting for our turn to speak.

Mindful communication begins with the intention to be fully present in the conversation. It requires us to let go of the need to multitask or constantly check our devices, and instead, prioritize the person in front of us. By giving our undivided attention, we create a space for deep connection and meaningful dialogue.

One of the key elements of mindful communication is active listening. When we actively listen, we are fully engaged in the conversation, focusing on the speaker's words, tone, and body language. We refrain from interrupting or jumping to conclusions and instead, seek to understand the speaker's perspective and experiences.

Mindful communication also involves cultivating empathy and compassion. It requires us to put ourselves in the shoes of the other person, seeking to understand their feelings, needs, and desires. By approaching conversations with empathy, we create an atmosphere of trust and openness, where authentic connections can thrive.

In addition to listening and empathy, mindful communication encourages us to choose our words thoughtfully and mindfully. It invites us to speak with intention, clarity, and kindness. Instead of reacting impulsively or speaking without considering the impact of our words, we take a moment to pause, reflect, and respond in a way that is respectful and compassionate.

Furthermore, mindful communication extends beyond verbal interactions. It encompasses nonverbal communication as well— our body language, facial expressions, and gestures. Being aware of our nonverbal cues and consciously aligning them with our words and intentions enhances the authenticity and effectiveness of our communication.

To cultivate mindful communication and presence in your interactions, start by creating a supportive environment that fosters open and honest dialogue. Choose spaces that are free from distractions and interruptions, where both parties can feel comfortable and heard.

Practice active listening by giving your full attention to the speaker. Maintain eye contact, nod in acknowledgment, and use verbal and nonverbal cues to show that you are engaged and attentive. Avoid the temptation to interrupt or formulate your response while the other person is speaking. Instead, listen with curiosity and seek to understand their perspective.

Cultivate empathy by putting yourself in the other person's shoes. Try to see the situation from their point of view and acknowledge their emotions and experiences. Respond with compassion and understanding, even if you may not agree with their perspective.

Choose your words carefully, considering their impact on the listener. Speak with clarity and honesty, expressing yourself authentically and respectfully. Be mindful of the tone of your voice and the nonverbal messages you convey, ensuring they align with your intended message.

Practice patience and give yourself and others the space to express themselves fully. Avoid rushing or interrupting conversations and allow for pauses and moments of reflection. These pauses can provide valuable insights and allow for deeper understanding to emerge.

Remember, mindful communication is a practice—an ongoing journey of self-awareness and growth. By embracing mindful communication and presence in your interactions, you create a foundation of respect, understanding, and connection. You foster deeper relationships, cultivate empathy, and contribute to a more harmonious and compassionate world.

CHAPTER 7:
EMBRACING SLOW
TRAVEL AND NATURE

I n a world that moves at a dizzying pace, where travel often involves rushing from one destination to another, and where nature is often overlooked amidst the chaos of modern life, it is essential to pause, take a deep breath, and reconnect with the beauty and tranquility that lie beyond our everyday routines. In this chapter, we delve into the transformative power of slow travel and the healing embrace of nature.

Slow travel is not merely about ticking off popular tourist attractions or rushing through a checklist of sights. It is a mindset —a way of approaching travel with intention, curiosity, and a willingness to immerse ourselves fully in the places we visit. Slow travel allows us to connect deeply with the local culture, engage with the communities we encounter, and create meaningful memories that will last a lifetime.

Nature, with its awe-inspiring landscapes, rejuvenating qualities, and profound wisdom, is a powerful antidote to the stresses and demands of modern life. When we embrace nature, we open ourselves up to its healing embrace, reconnecting with our innate sense of wonder, and rediscovering our place within the web of life. Nature beckons us to slow down, to listen to the whisper of the wind, to marvel at the dance of sunlight through the trees, and to find solace in the rhythms of the natural world.

In this chapter, we will explore the art of slow travel and the profound benefits of immersing ourselves in nature. We will discover how to cultivate a mindset of presence and curiosity while exploring new destinations. We will learn to approach travel with a sense of mindfulness, cherishing the journey as much as the destination itself. We will also uncover the transformative power of nature, and how it can provide us with solace, inspiration, and a deeper connection to the world around us.

Through slow travel, we have the opportunity to break free from the hurried pace of modern tourism and to forge authentic connections with the places we visit. We can engage in meaningful cultural exchanges, support local communities, and create lasting memories that go beyond mere snapshots. Slow travel invites us to wander off the beaten path, to embrace serendipitous encounters, and to cultivate a sense of wonder and awe as we explore the world.

Nature, on the other hand, invites us to slow down and listen. It reminds us of our interdependence with the Earth and the need to protect and preserve its beauty. By immersing ourselves in nature, we can experience moments of profound stillness, find solace in its simplicity, and reconnect with our own inner essence.

So, as we embark on this chapter, let us open our hearts and minds to the transformative power of slow travel and nature. Let us embrace the art of mindful exploration, where each step is a celebration of the present moment. Let us surrender to the beauty and wisdom of the natural world, allowing it to guide us towards a deeper sense of connection, meaning, and harmony.

Get ready to embark on a journey of slow travel and immerse yourself in the healing embrace of nature. Let us wander, let us marvel, and let us rediscover the joy of being fully present in the world.

Discovering the Joy of Slow Travel and Immersing Yourself in New Cultures

Slow travel offers a unique opportunity to discover the joy of immersing yourself in new cultures, allowing you to go beyond mere surface-level interactions and truly connect with the essence of a place and its people. It is a transformative experience that encourages us to embrace a more intentional and immersive approach to travel, fostering a deeper understanding and appreciation of the diverse cultures that exist in our world.

When we embark on a journey of slow travel, we shed the role of a passive observer and become active participants in the cultures we encounter. We open ourselves up to new experiences, perspectives, and ways of life. By immersing ourselves in local traditions, customs, and rituals, we gain a profound understanding of the rich tapestry that makes each culture unique.

Immersing ourselves in a new culture requires an open mind and a willingness to step outside our comfort zones. It invites us to learn the language, engage with locals, and seek authentic experiences that go beyond the tourist veneer. Whether it's participating in a traditional ceremony, trying local cuisine, or learning traditional arts and crafts, slow travel allows us to peel back the layers and uncover the true essence of a culture.

One of the greatest joys of slow travel is the opportunity to forge meaningful connections with locals. By immersing ourselves in a culture, we can engage in heartfelt conversations, share stories, and learn from the wisdom and perspectives of the people we meet. These connections provide a deeper appreciation for the human experience, fostering empathy, understanding, and a sense of global interconnectedness.

In the pursuit of slow travel, we become cultural ambassadors, seeking not only to learn from others but also to share our own experiences and traditions. By engaging in cultural exchange, we create bridges of understanding and foster mutual respect and appreciation. Our interactions with locals become an exchange of ideas, traditions, and values, enriching both our own lives and the lives of those we meet along the way.

Immersing ourselves in new cultures also opens our hearts and minds to the beauty of diversity. We learn to celebrate the differences that make each culture unique and recognize the shared humanity that unites us all. Through this process, we become more tolerant, compassionate, and respectful global citizens.

To truly immerse yourself in a new culture during slow travel, take the time to engage with the local community. Seek out authentic experiences that showcase the traditions, art, music, and cuisine of the region. Participate in cultural events, visit local markets, and explore off-the-beaten-path neighborhoods. By stepping away from the tourist hubs and venturing into the heart of the local community, you will uncover hidden gems and create memories that will stay with you long after your journey ends.

Remember, slow travel is not about rushing from one famous landmark to another. It is about savoring the moments, embracing the unknown, and immersing yourself in the fabric of a culture. Take the time to listen to the stories of the locals, engage in meaningful conversations, and cultivate an attitude of respect and curiosity. By doing so, you will embark on a transformative journey of cultural exploration that will broaden your horizons, challenge your assumptions, and leave an indelible mark on your soul.

So, as you embrace the joy of slow travel, immerse yourself in the new cultures you encounter. Embrace the beauty of diversity, seek authentic experiences, and forge deep connections with the people you meet. Through this immersive approach, you will not only enrich your own life but also contribute to a world that celebrates and cherishes the cultural tapestry that binds us all together.

Connecting with Nature to Find Peace and Inspiration

Connecting with nature is a powerful way to find peace, inspiration, and a sense of harmony in our lives. In the midst of our fast-paced and technology-driven world, nature offers a sanctuary—a space where we can unplug, recharge, and reconnect with ourselves and the world around us.

When we immerse ourselves in nature, we tap into its inherent beauty and wisdom. We witness the cycles of life, the interdependence of all living beings, and the intricate balance of ecosystems. Nature teaches us the value of patience, resilience, and adaptability. It reminds us of our own place in the grand tapestry of life and instills a sense of humility and awe.

Nature has a profound ability to quiet the noise within us. As we breathe in the fresh air, listen to the rustle of leaves, and feel the gentle caress of a breeze, our minds begin to quiet, and our senses become attuned to the present moment. Nature invites us to let go of our worries, fears, and anxieties, and to fully embrace the serenity and stillness that surround us.

In nature, we find inspiration that fuels our creativity and ignites our imagination. The vastness of the sky, the majesty of mountains, the rhythm of waves crashing on the shore—all of these natural wonders stir something deep within us. They awaken our senses, open our minds, and invite us to see the world through a new lens. Whether it's a breathtaking sunset, a vibrant field of wildflowers, or the intricate patterns of a leaf, nature sparks our creativity and reminds us of the beauty that exists in the simplest of things.

Connecting with nature also offers us an opportunity for reflection and self-discovery. In the quiet solitude of a forest, by the side of a tranquil lake, or on a mountaintop, we can turn inward and listen to the whispers of our own hearts. Nature acts as a mirror, reflecting back our true essence and reminding us of what truly matters. It allows us to gain perspective, find clarity, and nurture our inner growth.

Moreover, spending time in nature has been shown to have numerous physical and mental health benefits. It reduces stress, lowers blood pressure, boosts immune function, and enhances overall well-being. The sights, sounds, and smells of nature have a soothing effect on our nervous system, promoting relaxation and rejuvenation. Whether it's taking a leisurely walk in a park, practicing yoga in a meadow, or simply sitting beneath a tree, nature offers us a natural remedy for the stresses of modern life.

To connect with nature and find peace and inspiration, make it a priority to spend time outdoors regularly. Take a walk in a nearby park, hike in a forest, or sit by the ocean. Engage your senses by observing the colors, textures, and sounds of nature. Practice mindfulness as you immerse yourself in the present moment, fully experiencing the beauty and tranquility that surrounds you.

Create rituals that deepen your connection with nature, such as sunrise or sunset meditations, journaling in a natural setting, or practicing outdoor yoga or tai chi. Engage in activities that allow you to explore and appreciate the wonders of the natural world, such as birdwatching, gardening, or photography.

Remember, nature is not separate from us—it is an integral part of who we are. By connecting with nature, we reconnect with ourselves and our own innate wisdom. We tap into a wellspring of inspiration, peace, and serenity that exists within us and all around us. So, let nature be your guide, your healer, and your source of inspiration as you embark on a journey of connection and self-discovery.

CHAPTER 8:
BALANCING WORK
AND LEISURE

I n our fast-paced and productivity-driven society, finding
a balance between work and leisure can be a significant
challenge. The demands of our careers, coupled with the
constant connectivity of technology, often blur the boundaries
between our professional and personal lives. As a result, we may
find ourselves trapped in a never-ending cycle of work, feeling
overwhelmed, stressed, and disconnected from the joys of leisure.
In this chapter, we will explore the importance of striking a
balance between work and leisure and provide practical strategies
for achieving harmony in this vital aspect of slow living.

Achieving a healthy work-life balance is crucial for our
overall well-being and happiness. It allows us to nurture our
relationships, pursue our passions, and recharge our energy,
leading to greater fulfillment and a more sustainable approach
to life. By prioritizing leisure and consciously setting boundaries
around work, we can reclaim our time and create space for the
activities that bring us joy, relaxation, and personal growth.

This chapter will delve into various aspects of balancing work
and leisure, offering insights and strategies to help you find

equilibrium in your daily life. From setting realistic expectations and establishing boundaries to embracing the concept of rest and rejuvenation, we will explore practical steps to enhance your work-life balance and create a more fulfilling and sustainable lifestyle.

We will also explore the concept of mindful productivity, which involves cultivating a focused and purposeful approach to work, optimizing efficiency, and embracing the principles of slow living. By practicing mindful productivity, you can streamline your work processes, reduce stress, and create more time for leisure and self-care.

Furthermore, we will discuss the importance of leisure activities and the role they play in enhancing our overall well-being. Engaging in hobbies, pursuing creative endeavors, and spending quality time with loved ones are all essential components of a balanced life. We will explore ways to incorporate these activities into your schedule, prioritize self-care, and create a fulfilling leisure time that nourishes your mind, body, and soul.

Balancing work and leisure is a continuous journey that requires reflection, self-awareness, and ongoing adjustments. It involves aligning your values and priorities, learning to say no to excessive demands, and embracing a more intentional and mindful approach to both work and leisure. By integrating the principles of slow living into your daily routine, you can create a harmonious balance that allows you to thrive in all areas of your life.

In the chapters that follow, we will delve deeper into the strategies, practices, and mindset shifts necessary to achieve a meaningful and sustainable balance between work and leisure. Through mindful presence, conscious choices, and a commitment to your well-being, you can transform your relationship with work, nurture your personal life, and embrace a more fulfilling and balanced way of living.

Examining Your Relationship with Work and Finding a Healthy Balance

Our relationship with work greatly influences our overall well-being and quality of life. For many of us, work occupies a significant portion of our time and energy, making it crucial to examine our relationship with work and strive for a healthy balance. In this subchapter, we will explore the importance of evaluating your relationship with work and provide guidance on finding a sustainable and fulfilling balance.

Reflect on your values and priorities

Take a moment to reflect on your values and priorities in life. Consider what truly matters to you beyond your professional aspirations. Is it spending quality time with loved ones, pursuing personal passions, or maintaining good physical and mental health? By gaining clarity on your values, you can align your work-life balance accordingly and make conscious decisions that honor your priorities.

Assess your work expectations

Examine the expectations you have set for yourself in your professional life. Are you constantly striving for perfection, working long hours, or neglecting other areas of your life in pursuit of career success? It's essential to reassess these expectations and question whether they are realistic and sustainable. Set realistic goals and establish boundaries to prevent work from overshadowing other essential aspects of your life.

Establish boundaries

Boundaries are vital in maintaining a healthy work-life balance. Clearly define your working hours, and communicate these boundaries to your colleagues and clients. Resist the temptation to be constantly available and learn to disconnect from work during your designated personal time. Establishing boundaries ensures that you have dedicated time for leisure, rest, and activities that nurture your well-being.

Practice work-life integration

Instead of striving for a strict separation between work and personal life, consider adopting a more integrated approach. Look for ways to blend work and leisure by incorporating activities that bring you joy and relaxation into your workday. This could include taking short breaks to engage in mindfulness exercises, going for a walk during lunchtime, or finding moments of creativity amidst your work tasks. Integrating work and leisure can lead to a more balanced and fulfilling experience.

Seek flexibility

Whenever possible, seek flexibility in your work arrangements. This could mean negotiating flexible working hours, exploring remote work options, or creating a schedule that allows for a healthy balance between work and personal commitments. Flexibility enables you to adapt to the changing demands of your life and promotes a greater sense of autonomy and well-being.

Prioritize self-care

Self-care is essential for maintaining a healthy work-life balance. Make self-care practices a non-negotiable part of your routine. Prioritize activities that promote relaxation, stress reduction, and rejuvenation, such as exercise, meditation, hobbies, or spending time in nature. By taking care of your physical, emotional, and mental well-being, you'll be better equipped to manage the demands of work and find greater satisfaction in all areas of your life.

Seek support and collaboration

Don't be afraid to seek support from colleagues, friends, and family. Delegate tasks, ask for help when needed, and cultivate a support system that can assist you in balancing your work and personal responsibilities. Collaboration and teamwork can alleviate the burden of work and create a more harmonious and efficient work environment.

Finding a healthy balance between work and other aspects of

1234567890123456123456789012345678901234567890123123456789011234567890123456781234567890112345678901212345678901212345678901234

123456789012123456789012312345678901234567890112341234567123456121234512345

X

Create a conducive environment

Designate a space or create an environment that is conducive to pursuing your passions and hobbies. Whether it's a cozy reading nook, a well-equipped workshop, or a serene garden, having a space that is tailored to your interests can enhance your enjoyment and focus. Surround yourself with the tools, materials, or equipment you need to fully immerse yourself in your chosen activities.

Start small and be consistent

It's not necessary to devote hours upon hours to your hobbies every day. Start small and be consistent. Even dedicating a few minutes each day or setting aside a couple of hours per week can make a significant difference. Consistency is key. By consistently engaging in your passions and hobbies, you deepen your skills, experience progress, and derive greater satisfaction from the activities.

Embrace the learning process

Embrace the learning process that comes with nurturing your passions and hobbies. Recognize that you don't have to be an expert from the start. Embrace the beginner's mindset and allow yourself to make mistakes and learn from them. Enjoy the journey of growth and discovery as you develop new skills, expand your knowledge, and explore different facets of your interests.

Seek inspiration and community

Seek inspiration from others who share similar passions or hobbies. Join clubs, classes, or online communities where you can connect with like-minded individuals, exchange ideas, and receive support and encouragement. Engaging with others who share your interests can foster a sense of belonging and provide valuable opportunities for collaboration and learning.

Embrace creativity and playfulness

When nurturing your passions and hobbies, embrace a sense of creativity and playfulness. Allow yourself to experiment, think outside the box, and explore different approaches or techniques. Playfulness stimulates your imagination, ignites your creativity, and adds a sense of joy and freedom to your leisure pursuits.

Remember, your passions and hobbies are not mere distractions from work or responsibilities; they are essential components of a balanced and fulfilling life. By actively nurturing your passions and hobbies, you infuse your leisure time with purpose, self-expression, and personal growth. They provide a counterbalance to the demands of daily life, promote a sense of fulfillment, and contribute to your overall well-being. So, make time for what brings you joy, explore your interests, and cultivate a more meaningful and satisfying leisure time.

CHAPTER 9: EMBRACING SIMPLICITY IN TECHNOLOGY

In our modern world, technology has become an integral part of our lives. It has revolutionized the way we work, communicate, and access information. While technology offers numerous benefits and conveniences, it can also contribute to a sense of overwhelm, distraction, and disconnection if not approached mindfully. In this chapter, we will explore the concept of embracing simplicity in technology and how it can help us regain control, find balance, and enhance our overall well-being.

In today's digital age, we are constantly bombarded with notifications, alerts, and an endless stream of information. Our devices can easily become a source of stress and distraction, pulling us away from the present moment and impeding our ability to engage fully with our surroundings and ourselves. Embracing simplicity in technology does not mean rejecting it entirely; rather, it involves adopting a more intentional and mindful approach to how we interact with and use technology.

By embracing simplicity in technology, we can reclaim our time, attention, and focus. We can create a healthier relationship with our devices, leveraging their benefits while minimizing the negative impact they may have on our well-being. In this chapter, we will explore practical strategies and mindset shifts that can help us navigate the digital landscape with intention and purpose.

We will delve into the following key areas:

Assessing and streamlining digital clutter
We will discuss the importance of evaluating our digital environments, such as our inboxes, social media accounts, and digital files. We will explore strategies for decluttering, organizing, and streamlining our digital spaces to create a more peaceful and focused digital experience.

Practicing mindful technology use
We will explore the concept of mindful technology use, which involves being fully present and aware of our interactions with technology. We will discuss techniques for setting boundaries, managing notifications, and developing a more conscious and intentional relationship with our devices.

Cultivating digital well-being habits
We will delve into the importance of cultivating healthy digital habits that promote balance and well-being. We will explore practices such as digital detoxes, establishing tech-free zones or times, and finding alternative activities that nourish our minds, bodies, and relationships.

Nurturing digital mindfulness
We will explore techniques for cultivating digital mindfulness, which involves bringing awareness, intention, and compassion to our digital experiences. We will discuss strategies for being more present, practicing digital self-care, and fostering meaningful connections in our online interactions.

Harnessing technology for intentional living

Finally, we will explore ways to leverage technology to support our slow living journey and enhance our overall well-being. We will discuss tools and apps that can help us with mindfulness, productivity, and intentional living, as well as tips for using technology to foster creativity, learning, and personal growth.

By embracing simplicity in technology, we can reclaim our digital lives and use technology as a tool to enhance our well-being and support our slow living ideals. It is about taking conscious control of our digital experiences, finding balance, and using technology in ways that align with our values and priorities. Let us embark on this chapter with an open mind, ready to explore how we can create a healthier, more intentional relationship with technology in our fast-paced digital world.

Mindful Use of Technology to Enhance Rather Than Dominate Your Life

In today's digital age, technology has permeated nearly every aspect of our lives. From smartphones to laptops, social media to streaming services, we are constantly surrounded by digital devices and platforms. While technology offers countless benefits and conveniences, it can also easily take over our lives, leaving us feeling overwhelmed, disconnected, and consumed by screens.

However, by cultivating a mindful approach to technology, we can harness its potential to enhance our lives rather than dominate them. Mindful use of technology involves being intentional, present, and aware of our digital interactions. It empowers us to take control of our relationship with technology, creating boundaries, and using it in ways that align with our values and priorities. In this subchapter, we will explore strategies for cultivating mindful use of technology to enhance our overall well-being.

Define your digital boundaries
Start by defining clear boundaries around your technology use.

Reflect on how much time you want to allocate to different activities, such as work, leisure, and personal connections. Set limits on the amount of screen time you allow yourself each day and establish specific times or zones where you are device-free. By setting boundaries, you create space for other meaningful activities and foster a healthier balance in your life.

Practice digital mindfulness

Incorporate mindfulness into your digital experiences. Before engaging with technology, take a moment to check in with yourself. Notice your intentions and emotions. Are you seeking connection, information, or entertainment? Be aware of how you feel during and after using technology. Are you experiencing joy, inspiration, or overwhelm? By practicing digital mindfulness, you develop a greater sense of self-awareness and can make conscious choices about how you engage with technology.

Curate your digital environment

Take a proactive approach to curating your digital environment. Evaluate the apps, social media accounts, and online communities you participate in. Are they adding value to your life? Do they align with your values and interests? Consider unfollowing accounts that trigger negative emotions or create a sense of comparison. Surround yourself with digital content that inspires and uplifts you. By curating your digital environment, you create a space that supports your well-being and aligns with your intentions.

Limit notifications and distractions

Notifications can disrupt our focus and pull us away from the present moment. Take control of your notifications by turning off or limiting non-essential ones. Determine specific times when you will check emails, messages, or social media instead of constantly being at the mercy of incoming notifications. Minimize distractions by using tools that block or limit access to certain websites or apps during focused work or leisure time. By reducing digital interruptions, you can cultivate deeper focus and be more present in your activities.

Engage with technology mindfully
As you engage with technology, practice mindfulness. Notice your posture, breathing, and bodily sensations. Are you tensing up, hunching over, or holding your breath? Take regular breaks to stretch, move, and rest your eyes. Be mindful of your digital consumption habits, avoiding mindless scrolling or binge-watching. Instead, choose activities that align with your values and support your well-being, such as learning, creating, or connecting with loved ones.

Foster offline connections and activities
While technology can facilitate connections, it is important not to neglect the value of offline interactions. Make time for face-to-face conversations, engaging in hobbies, or enjoying nature without the presence of digital devices. Prioritize quality time with loved ones, creating opportunities for deeper connections and meaningful experiences. By nurturing offline connections and activities, you cultivate a more balanced and fulfilling life.

Remember, technology is a tool that should serve us, not dominate us. By embracing mindful use of technology, we can harness its benefits while staying connected to ourselves and the world around us. It's about finding a harmonious balance between the digital and analog aspects of our lives and using technology in ways that enhance our well-being and support our slow living journey. Let us embark on this mindful approach to technology, reclaiming control, and cultivating a healthier relationship with the digital world.

Cultivating Digital Boundaries and Fostering Healthy Tech Habits

In our digitally connected world, it's essential to establish clear boundaries and foster healthy habits when it comes to our technology use. Without conscious awareness and intentional choices, technology can easily encroach upon our lives, leading to feelings of overwhelm, distraction, and diminished well-being. In this subchapter, we will explore practical strategies for cultivating digital boundaries and fostering healthy tech habits that support our slow living journey.

Define your digital boundaries

Start by clarifying your personal boundaries around technology use. Reflect on the areas of your life where you want to set limits and establish guidelines. Consider designating tech-free zones or times, such as during meals, before bed, or during specific activities like reading or spending quality time with loved ones. By defining clear boundaries, you create space for other aspects of your life and protect your well-being.

Set screen time limits

One effective way to cultivate healthy tech habits is by setting limits on your screen time. Determine how much time you want to spend engaging with screens each day and establish a schedule or routine that allows for dedicated screen-free periods. Use apps or features on your devices that track and manage your screen time, providing you with insights into your digital habits and helping you stay accountable to your goals.

Practice digital detoxes

Periodically disconnecting from technology can be a powerful way to reset and recharge. Consider incorporating digital detoxes into your routine, whether it's for a few hours, a day, a weekend, or longer. During this time, abstain from using devices and engage in activities that promote relaxation, creativity, and connection with the offline world. Use this opportunity to focus on self-care, pursue hobbies, and spend quality time with loved ones.

Establish tech-free rituals

Introduce tech-free rituals into your daily life to create intentional breaks from digital distractions. This could be as simple as starting your day with a mindful morning routine before checking your phone or implementing a digital curfew in the evening to ensure quality rest. Engage in activities that bring you joy and nourish your well-being, such as reading a physical book, practicing yoga or meditation, or enjoying nature.

Practice mindful tech consumption

Be mindful of how you consume digital content and engage with technology. Avoid mindless scrolling or getting caught in the rabbit hole of endless distractions. Instead, practice conscious and purposeful consumption. Before clicking on a link or opening an app, ask yourself if it aligns with your values, priorities, or current intentions. Set specific goals for your online activities and be selective about the information and media you consume.

Establish tech-free social interactions

Nurture your relationships by fostering tech-free social interactions. When spending time with loved ones or engaging in social gatherings, prioritize being fully present and attentive. Create tech-free zones during social events or meals, encouraging meaningful conversations and genuine connections. By setting these boundaries, you can deepen your relationships and cultivate more fulfilling social experiences.

Practice digital well-being rituals

Incorporate digital well-being rituals into your daily routine. This may include taking regular breaks from screens to stretch, move your body, or practice deep breathing. Explore mindfulness or meditation apps that help you disconnect from the digital noise and reconnect with yourself. Prioritize activities that promote self-care and reduce the negative impact of technology on your well-being.

Remember, cultivating digital boundaries and fostering healthy tech habits is about taking control of your digital experiences and aligning them with your values and priorities. By consciously engaging with technology, you create space for more meaningful connections, activities, and moments of presence in your life.

Embrace the power of intentionality and let technology serve as a supportive tool on your slow living journey.

CHAPTER 10:
CULTIVATING INNER
STILLNESS

In the midst of a fast-paced and chaotic world, finding moments of inner stillness has become a rare and precious commodity. Our lives are filled with constant noise, distractions, and demands that can leave us feeling overwhelmed, scattered, and disconnected from ourselves. However, within each of us lies the potential to cultivate a deep sense of inner stillness, tranquility, and peace.

In this chapter, we will explore the art of cultivating inner stillness as a foundational practice for slow living. We will delve into various techniques and approaches that can help us quiet the mind, anchor ourselves in the present moment, and tap into a profound sense of inner calm. By nurturing this inner stillness, we can navigate life's challenges with greater clarity, resilience, and authenticity.

In a world that values constant activity and external achievements, cultivating inner stillness may seem counterintuitive. However, it is within these moments of stillness that we can reconnect with our true selves, our inner wisdom, and the deeper currents of life. It is a deliberate act of slowing down, tuning in, and creating space for reflection, introspection, and self-discovery.

Throughout this chapter, we will explore a variety of practices and perspectives that can support the cultivation of inner stillness. From mindfulness meditation to breathwork, from nature immersion to journaling, each approach offers a unique pathway to quieting the mind and accessing a state of inner peace. By experimenting with different techniques and finding what resonates with us individually, we can develop a personal toolkit for cultivating inner stillness.

Cultivating inner stillness is not about escaping from the world or avoiding its challenges. Rather, it is a practice that allows us to engage with life from a place of greater centeredness, clarity, and authenticity. It is about creating a sanctuary within ourselves—a sacred space where we can find solace, recharge our energies, and connect with our deepest aspirations and values.

As we embark on this journey of cultivating inner stillness, let us embrace the power of silence, solitude, and self-reflection. Let us create intentional pauses in our lives, where we can detach from the noise and distractions of the external world and listen deeply to the whispers of our hearts. Through the practice of inner stillness, we can reclaim our inner resources, nourish our souls, and find a profound sense of peace and purpose.

So, let us begin this exploration of cultivating inner stillness, knowing that the journey may not always be easy, but the rewards are immeasurable. As we invite more moments of quiet into our lives, we open ourselves to the transformative power of stillness and embark on a path of deeper self-awareness, self-compassion, and spiritual growth. Together, let us embrace the practice of cultivating inner stillness as an essential pillar of our slow living journey.

Finding Moments of Silence and Solitude

for Reflection and Self-Discovery

In a world filled with noise, constant stimulation, and external demands, intentionally carving out moments of silence and solitude becomes an essential practice for cultivating inner stillness and fostering self-discovery. These precious moments offer us an opportunity to disconnect from the external world, quiet the mind, and tune into our inner landscape. In this subchapter, we will explore the significance of finding moments of silence and solitude and discover practical ways to incorporate them into our lives.

Embracing the power of silence

Silence holds a profound energy that can nourish our souls and foster deep self-reflection. Finding moments of silence allows us to step away from the constant chatter of our minds and the external noise, creating a space for inner peace and clarity. It can be as simple as sitting in a quiet room, taking a silent walk in nature, or practicing silent meditation. Embrace the power of silence as a gateway to self-discovery and inner stillness.

Creating intentional alone time

Solitude provides an opportunity to reconnect with ourselves, away from the distractions and influences of others. It allows us to explore our thoughts, emotions, and desires in a safe and private space. Designate specific periods of alone time in your schedule—a daily ritual, a weekend getaway, or even a solitary retreat. Use this time to engage in activities that bring you joy, such as journaling, creative pursuits, or simply being present with yourself.

Disconnecting from technology

In our hyperconnected world, technology often fills every available moment. However, finding silence and solitude requires disconnecting from the constant stream of digital notifications and distractions. Set aside dedicated periods of technology-free time to unplug and create a digital sanctuary. Put your devices on silent, limit social media use, and resist the urge to constantly check emails or messages. Instead, use this time to be fully present, reconnect with yourself, and engage in offline activities that nourish your well-being.

Engaging in mindful practices

Mindfulness is a powerful tool for cultivating inner stillness and self-discovery. By bringing our attention to the present moment, we can quiet the mental chatter and deepen our connection with ourselves. Incorporate mindfulness practices such as meditation, deep breathing exercises, or mindful movement into your routine. These practices anchor us in the here and now, creating a space for self-reflection and insight.

Seeking nature's embrace

Nature provides a tranquil and nourishing backdrop for moments of silence and solitude. Spend time in natural surroundings—whether it's a local park, a forest, a beach, or a mountainside. Allow yourself to fully immerse in the beauty and serenity of nature. Engage your senses, observe the intricate details, and feel the grounding presence of the natural world. As you connect with nature, you create a space for inner stillness, reflection, and a deeper sense of connection to the world around you.

Cultivating a reflective practice

Incorporate reflective practices into your moments of silence and solitude. Journaling, self-inquiry exercises, or engaging in meaningful conversations with yourself can help deepen your self-awareness and facilitate self-discovery. Use these practices to explore your thoughts, emotions, dreams, and aspirations. Ask yourself meaningful questions and allow the answers to emerge naturally. Reflective practices provide a gateway to understanding yourself on a deeper level and uncovering insights that can guide your slow living journey.

By intentionally finding moments of silence and solitude, we create a sanctuary for self-discovery, reflection, and inner stillness. These moments allow us to listen to our inner voice, access our intuition, and gain clarity about our values, desires, and aspirations. Embrace the power of silence and solitude as transformative tools for nurturing your inner world and fostering a deep connection to yourself. As you cultivate these moments in your life, you will experience a greater sense of inner peace, self-awareness, and a profound alignment with your slow living values.

Tapping into Your Inner Wisdom and Intuition

Within each of us lies a wellspring of wisdom and intuition, waiting to be tapped into. In the midst of our busy lives, it can be easy to overlook this inner guidance and rely solely on external sources of information and validation. However, by intentionally cultivating a connection with our inner wisdom and intuition, we can make more aligned and authentic decisions, navigate challenges with greater ease, and find deeper meaning and fulfillment in our lives. In this subchapter, we will explore ways to tap into your inner wisdom and intuition.

Cultivate self-awareness

Self-awareness is the foundation for accessing your inner wisdom and intuition. Take time to explore your thoughts, emotions, and beliefs. Notice how your body responds to different situations. Pay attention to your inner voice and the messages it conveys. Engage in practices such as meditation, mindfulness, and journaling to deepen your self-awareness and strengthen your connection with your inner world.

Trust your gut feelings

Often referred to as a "gut feeling" or "intuition," our inner knowing is a powerful source of wisdom. It is that subtle sense of knowing without logical explanation. Practice tuning in to your gut feelings and honoring them. When faced with a decision, pause and listen to what your intuition is telling you. Trust that your inner wisdom knows what is best for you, even if it doesn't align with external expectations or rational reasoning.

Embrace stillness and silence
Creating moments of stillness and silence allows space for your inner wisdom to emerge. Set aside time each day to be in quiet contemplation. It could be in the form of meditation, sitting in nature, or simply finding a peaceful spot in your home. As you quiet the external noise, you create a fertile ground for your inner wisdom to rise to the surface.

Practice mindfulness
Mindfulness is a powerful practice for cultivating presence and accessing your inner wisdom. By bringing your full attention to the present moment, you become more attuned to your thoughts, emotions, and sensations. Practice mindful awareness in your daily activities, such as eating, walking, or engaging in conversations. As you develop a habit of mindfulness, you become more receptive to the subtle insights and guidance that arise from within.

Engage in creative expression
Creativity is a doorway to the realm of intuition and inner wisdom. Engaging in creative pursuits, such as painting, writing, dancing, or playing an instrument, allows you to tap into a deeper part of yourself. Give yourself permission to express without judgment or attachment to outcomes. Allow your creativity to flow freely, and observe the insights and wisdom that emerge through the process.

Seek solitude in nature
Nature has a way of quieting the mind and opening the channels of intuition. Spend time in natural environments, whether it's a park, garden, or wilderness area. Allow yourself to connect with the natural world, observe its rhythms, and attune yourself to its wisdom. Nature has a way of reminding us of our interconnectedness and can serve as a powerful ally in accessing our inner wisdom and intuition.

Practice intuitive journaling

Journaling can be a powerful tool for tapping into your inner wisdom. Set aside time for reflective writing, where you allow your thoughts and feelings to flow freely onto the page. Ask open-ended questions and let the answers emerge naturally. Trust the insights that come through your writing and use them as guidance in your slow living journey.

Remember, accessing your inner wisdom and intuition is a journey of deepening self-trust and cultivating a greater connection with yourself. It requires creating space for stillness, listening to the whispers of your intuition, and honoring the wisdom that arises from within. As you embrace this practice, you will find yourself making decisions that are in alignment with your true desires and values, and living a more authentic and fulfilling life.

CONCLUSION

In this book, we embarked on a journey to explore the art of slow living—a mindful and intentional way of embracing life's rhythms, savoring the present moment, and finding balance and fulfillment in a fast-paced world. We delved into various aspects of slow living, from unveiling its origins and principles to cultivating mindfulness, creating tranquil homes, nourishing our bodies with slow food, prioritizing self-care, and fostering meaningful connections.

Throughout our exploration, we discovered that slow living is not about doing everything at a snail's pace or abandoning our responsibilities. It is about approaching life with a sense of intention, presence, and authenticity. It is about recognizing the need to step away from the culture of busyness, redefining success on our own terms, and prioritizing what truly matters to us.

We learned the importance of cultivating mindful awareness, embracing gratitude, and finding joy in everyday moments. We explored the significance of creating tranquil spaces that support our well-being and nourish our souls. We discovered the power of slow food—mindful eating and sustainable choices that not only nourish our bodies but also honor the earth and its resources.

In our journey of slow living, we realized the vital role of self-care in nurturing our physical, emotional, and mental well-being. We explored the transformative power of meaningful connections—

with loved ones, nature, and ourselves. We learned to balance work and leisure, to nurture our passions and hobbies, and to find fulfillment outside the realm of productivity.

We also delved into the realm of technology, learning to use it mindfully and establish healthy boundaries. We discovered the value of silence, solitude, and tapping into our inner wisdom and intuition. And throughout this journey, we recognized the beauty of simplicity, the joy of living at a slower pace, and the freedom that comes with aligning our lives with our values.

As we conclude this book, remember that slow living is not a destination but a lifelong journey. It is a continuous practice of self-reflection, intentionality, and choosing what truly matters to us. It is about embracing the beauty of simplicity, savoring the richness of each moment, and creating a life that aligns with our deepest values and aspirations.

May the wisdom and insights gained from this book inspire you to embrace slow living in your own unique way. May you find moments of stillness, presence, and connection in the midst of life's busyness. May you prioritize self-care, nurture meaningful relationships, and cultivate a deep appreciation for the simple joys of life. And may slow living guide you towards a more fulfilling, balanced, and meaningful existence.

Embrace the journey of slow living, and let it lead you to a life of purpose, authenticity, and deep contentment.

Printed in Great Britain
by Amazon

41132550R00046